AZU's Dreams of Thailand
Chiang Mai
Published in 2005 by AZU Editions Ltd.
13/F, Silver Fortune Plaza
1 Wellington Street
Central, Hong Kong
www.azueditions.com

Produced by ink it Group Co. Ltd.
111 SKV Building, 3/F
Soi Sansabai, Sukhumvit Soi 36
Klongton, Klongtoey
Bangkok 10110, Thailand
Tel: 66 (0) 2661 2893
Fax: 66 (0) 2661 6895
info@inkitgroup.com
www.inkitgroup.com

ISBN 988-98140-7-2

Printed in Thailand

Sponsored by

*Thai Airways International
Public Company Ltd.*

AZU'S
DREAMS OF THAILAND

Chiang Mai

Photographs by Marc Schultz
Text by John Hoskin

AZU

Rose of the North was the old soubriquet for

Chiang Mai. In recent years, Thailand's second city and former capital of the ancient Lanna kingdom has outgrown such a connotation of the rural, and yet it retains the essence more of a historic country town than of a modern urban hub.

This derives not simply from the preservation of a moat, old city gates and venerable temples, but more subtly from a unique character evolved through a separate historical development.

Founded in 1291 by King Mengrai as the capital of his Lanna kingdom, Chiang Mai pursued largely its own course down through the centuries. Although the Burmese took control of the city in the mid-1500s, political loss was cultural gain. The Thais of Lanna adopted, and adapted from their Burmese overlords, various influences, ranging from architecture to the culinary arts.

The Burmese were expelled from all Thai territory in the 18th century, but even then Chiang Mai retained a certain autonomy under the local rule of its own governor-prince, and it was not until the 1930s that the city was directly controlled by Bangkok.

A sense of security that comes with an identity defined over centuries is apparent today in the

people of Chiang Mai, who are more easy-going than their Bangkok counterparts. They also tend to cling more closely to traditional values, and are generally home-loving and unostentatious. Also, the custom of entering the monkhood is still widespread among boys and young men, and ordination ceremonies tend to be more elaborate than elsewhere in the Kingdom.

Festivities in general are again marked by greater panache and exuberance. Here the quintessential Thai trait of *sanuk*, having a good time, has not been diluted by the modern business ethic, and it's long been recognized that Chiang Mai is the place to celebrate Songkran, the merriest and most boisterous of all annual Thai festivals.

Speaking of having a good time, Chiang Mai further distinguishes itself in its northern cuisine. The Thais in general take great pleasure in eating and northerners are no exception, but their food is. Here the staple is not plain rice, as in most other parts of the country, but sticky or glutinous rice, eaten with a variety of fish and meat dishes which have a strong Burmese flavour and are remarkable even in a land renowned for its culinary arts.

Differences are again apparent in the sights that attract all travellers to Thailand – temples. Like Bangkok, Chiang Mai has its list of must-

sees – Wat Chiang Man, Wat Phra Singh, Wat Chedi Luang, Wat Suan Dok, Wat Chet Yot and the sublime hilltop Wat Phrathat Doi Suthep – but

these are much older than the Buddhist temples seen in the Thai capital, as well as being distinct in their architecture and adornment, particularly woodcarving.

Indeed, the people of Lanna have long excelled in arts and crafts, and traditional skills are alive and thriving. Woodcarving, silverware, pottery, lacquerware, weaving and, emblematic of Chiang Mai, paper umbrellas are all produced in artists' enclaves in and around the city. To stroll the streets, wander around the famed Night Bazaar and visit workshops is to discover a veritable Aladdin's cave of quality crafts both traditional in design and refashioned as modern décor items.

As pronounced as Chiang Mai's historical and cultural distinctions are, the impact of nature is

inescapable. The Ping River that flows through the city waters the Chiang Mai valley, turning it into lush fertile land yielding rich harvests. Beyond are high rolling hills, jungle-covered mountains, forests, waterfalls and caves. Adding intrigue to the landscape are the villages of several different hilltribes. Recognized by their colourful tribal costumes, these ethnic minorities continue to pursue independent lifestyles outside mainstream society.

Chiang Mai today is expanding and modernizing, yet one of the Kingdom's oldest continually inhabited cities does not relinquish a tenacious hold on its unique cultural heritage, nor turn its back on the grandeur of nature that characterizes its setting. A rose, as Gertrude Stein famously remarked, is a rose, is a rose.

16

54

Acknowledgements

The publisher would like to thank the following whose assistance has made this book possible:

Thai Airways International Public Co. Ltd., Ramita Saisuwan and Keith Mundy.

Photo Credits

The photographs in the book were taken by **Marc Schultz** with the exception of the following:

Dave Lloyd: 6, 12, 16, 17, 18-19, 28, 35, 46, 48, 49, 50

Nalinmard Sriphum: 2-3, 4, 7, 21, 22, 30-31, 36-37, 52-53, 56

Mark Standen: 38, 39, 47

Authors

Marc Schultz is a Bangkok-based American photographer with a passion for capturing scenes of traditional Thai life. When not documenting the idyllic traditional life of rural Thailand, Marc is a successful commercial photographer for both individual and corporate clients.

John Hoskin is an award-winning freelance travel writer who has been based in Thailand since 1979. He is the author of more than 20 books on travel, art and culture in Southeast Asia, and has had over 1,000 magazine articles published.